Axioms:

In Search of a Comprehensive Philosophy of Life

by Mounir Murad

Murad Publishing
Alexandria, Virginia

Murad Publishing
P.O. Box 16680
Alexandria, Virginia 22302-8680

Axioms strictly reflects the views of the author, and does not necessarily reflect the views of any organized religious, political, or social group of any kind.

Murad Publishing takes full responsibility for the contents, publishing, distributing, and marketing of this book.

Library of Congress Catalog Card No. 92-90950

Copyright ©1992 by Mounir Murad
ALL RIGHTS RESERVED

ISBN 0-9633519-6-6

Printed in the United States of America

To The Soul of the Beloved and Guiding Prophet

Since the beginning of time, and whether you descended to us in this world as Moses, David, Solomon, Christ, Mohammed, Dahesh or another, you have always taken the task of enlightening our souls at the expense of your pain and sorrow. It is with my deepest regard to your spirit that I write this book. If I have committed transgressions in some areas, I beg your forgiveness, for it is only stemming from my human ignorance. If I have not, then please consider it as a miniscule repayment of debt for what you have done for me.

ACKNOWLEDGMENTS

Many thanks to Marcia Whitmore for her assistance in editing this book. I would also like to thank my friend Jim Hopke for the many hours of interesting and enlightening discussions.

CONTENTS

Introduction **1**

Chapter 1: *Creator and Creation* **5**

Chapter 2: *Religions* **23**

Chapter 3: *Life and Death* **29**

Chapter 4: *Cause and Effect,
    Life's Realities and Ambiguities* **45**

Chapter 5: *The Final Days* **61**

INTRODUCTION

One of the things that troubles me most about human beings is their acceptance of things in life simply because that is the way they were raised to think. People accept many things as true, without proof, to form axioms —and they base their lives on these axioms. When people are confronted with questions that challenge their axioms, the most common answer they give is "I don't know!"

If science is capable of proving or disproving certain things, many of these axioms should no longer exist. But at no time soon is science likely to come up with answers to questions that pertain to our existence. So, for the time being, should we adhere to these unproven axioms, or should we attempt logically to find the most probable answers to our questions? Once we have formulated logical deductions, we can create a new set of axioms. The real question is are we ready to abandon our old axioms and accept new ones?

How do we deal with such issues as the presence of unequal suffering, fairness, wealth, and justice on Earth? Why are we born on Earth? Where are we going after death? Did we exist prior to our birth? What is the purpose of our creation? Is there a Creator? Is there life beyond this planet? Why is the Universe so vast? Why are we so much different from each other? Why are some people born with many talents, yet others are born retarded? Do we understand the reasons behind love and hatred? There are many other questions about life to which we seek answers.

If you are satisfied with the idea that life is wonderful and that the things mentioned earlier are of no importance to you, read no further. This book is not for you. But if you are dissatisfied with your life and would like to understand more about our existence, this book may provide some answers for you. It is not meant to solve all of your problems nor to explain all the mystical things in life; however, it may, I hope, serve to open your eyes so you can begin to question things that we otherwise take for granted.

When we are faced with a situation that warrants our analysis, do we rationalize, or do we look at the situation from the perspective of our religious beliefs? And if so, is this necessarily a bad thing to do? Are we so brainwashed or conditioned that we dismiss the resulting thoughts as being beyond our comprehension, brand them as "unexplainable," and move on without even attempting to find answers?

In my opinion, the moment we become satisfied with our existence and stop questioning the unexplainable phenomena that surround us is the moment of our intellectual death. Nothing short of a lifelong quest for the truth should be acceptable to us.

This book is a summary of my own personal quest. It is no secret that this quest of mine is heavily influenced by the "Daheshist" philosophical beliefs as I perceive them. You may read this book and say "This is nonsense!" Or you may concur with its philosophy or some part of it. No matter how you judge the book, it is my sincere wish that, after reading it, you will begin to view things from a wider and more logical perspective as you go through life.

CHAPTER 1

CREATOR AND CREATION

Is there a Creator? This is the most difficult of all questions. Can something be created from nothing? From the standpoint of science, the answer is no. For a new element to form, one or more existing elements must undergo change by exposure to external forces such as heat, electric current, light, pressure, atomic bombardment, or electron excitement. It is simply impossible to make matter appear out of nothing.

The Theory of Relativity draws a direct link between energy and mass; that is, mass can be changed into energy and vice versa according to the equation $E=mc^2$ (where E=energy, m=mass, and c=the speed of light). As expressed in this equation, the speed of light is a mathematical constant (300,000 Km/second); therefore, the only way for mass to exist is either through the conversion of energy, in accordance with the Theory of Relativity, or for both energy and mass to appear simultaneously from "nothing."

But if mass was created through the conversion of energy, where did this energy come from? Or if both mass and energy appeared simultaneously out of nothing, how did they come into existence? Suppose there is a force that could create energy or mass from nothing. Wouldn't scientists be forced to admit that such a force "defies the natural laws of the Universe?"

From the scientific viewpoint, everything in existence must have a beginning. If we try to trace its origin, sooner or later we will reach a dead end. For example, if we say that it is raining, we are implying that the evaporation of water from the Earth's surface causes a certain amount of moisture to develop in the atmosphere. This moisture is carried by air jets until it collides with a cold air front, which causes condensation that falls back to the surface of the Earth in the form of rain. This cycle repeats indefinitely as long as the conditions are appropriate. The question is how did the water come into existence? Which came first, the moisture in the atmosphere that condensed, or water that evaporated from seas and oceans? No matter which one we select as our answer, what created it?

If we talk about a new-born baby, we are indirectly talking about the product of a female egg and a male sperm. The question is this: Where did the first female egg and male sperm come from? Were they the product of a chemical reaction? If so, what elements were involved? What external forces were applied, and what created these elements? Even if we were able to discover their source, how was the first human being conceived without a womb? Which came first, the baby or the egg? If we say the egg, what created the egg? If we say the baby, what created the baby? If we say the first man and woman were not conceived but were created as living beings, we have just admitted that there is a Creator.

On a broader scale, if we look at our planet in reference to the Universe, we can say we are part of a solar system and that our sun is a star in a galaxy containing about 200,000,000,000 (200 billion) stars (see Figure 1).

Figure 1: Our sun is a star in a galaxy called the Milky Way that contains 200,000,000,000,000 (200 billion) stars. Our galaxy is one of thousands —or even millions— of galaxies that form the Universe.

NASA

7

We can also say that our galaxy is part of a supercluster that contains hundreds or even thousands of galaxies, that this supercluster is part of a universe which contains many superclusters, and that this universe is part of "?" It is this "?" that is so puzzling. If we assume that the "Big Bang" model is true and that the Universe was created by an explosion of some sort about 15,500,000,000 (15.5 billion) years ago, then *what* exploded in the Big Bang? How did *it* come into existence? Even if we were able to identify it, what created the creator of the thing that exploded in the Big Bang?

Let's take a closer look. Scientists believe that the Universe originated according to a model called the "Big Bang." This model theorized that the Universe is in a state of expansion and that galaxies are drifting apart in a uniform and predictable manner. Such expansion is not obvious to observers looking through telescopes; it takes millions of years to detect the evidence of such movement.

One of the methods scientists have used to detect this movement is spectral analysis, which has shown that all galaxies have shifted toward the red end of the spectrum. Such a red shift is indicative of an outward movement. By extrapolating this movement backward, these studies show the galaxies converging into a single source (see Figure 2).

If we could turn the clock backward, an old man would become middle-aged, then a young adult, then a teenager, a child, an infant, a fetus, and finally a sperm and egg. If we could turn the clock backward on the Universe, the galaxies would become closer and closer, until they all condense into one massive ball of gas and then merge. The term that is used to describe the origin

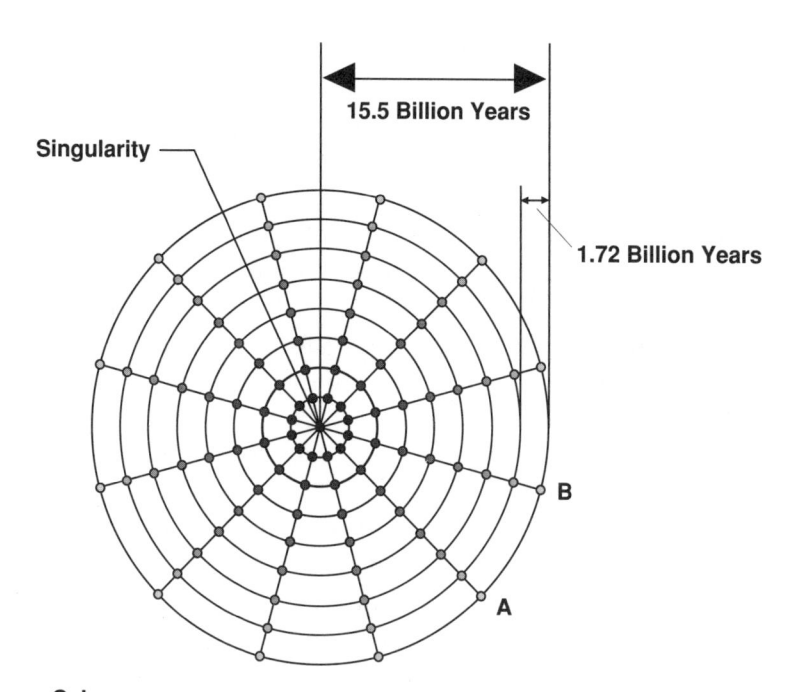

- **Galaxy**
  Different shades represent a shift of 1.72 billion years

Figure 2: Galaxy A and B converge into a single point (center) if we extrapolate their movement backward for about 15,500,000,000 (15.5 billion) years.

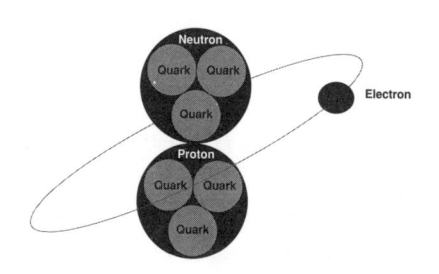

Figure 3: Components of a simple atom (Deuterium)

9

of the Universe from a single source —from this one massive ball of gas— is *singularity*. At that point, it is theorized that temperatures were so high that complex atoms could not form.

At about one second after the Big Bang and as we get closer to the moment of creation, the temperatures continue to rise to a point where the nuclei of all atoms break apart (10 billion degrees). At this point, matter exists in the form of particles, mainly electrons, protons, and neutrons. As we regress further in time, to a very small fraction of a second (10 microseconds or one millionth of a second) after the Big Bang, the protons and neutrons freed by the enormous temperatures (10 trillion degrees) break down into quarks, the smallest indivisible component of the atom (see Figure 3).

Many phenomena, such as the presence of background microwave radiation in space and space ripples, recently discovered by the Cosmic Background Explorer Satellite tend to support the validity of this theory. However, the basic theory does not sufficiently explain what happens infinitely approaching the zero point, regressing through time toward the moment of creation.

The Inflationary Universe model, an outgrowth of the Big Bang model, attempts to explain what happens infinitely nearing the zero point. This model is based upon the theory that there is a single force from which the four forces known to man developed: *gravity*; *weak force*, the force inside the nucleus responsible for radioactive decay; *electromagnetic force*; and *strong force*, the force inside the nucleus that acts to hold the nucleus together. This fundamental premise is referred to as the Grand Unified Theories of physics.

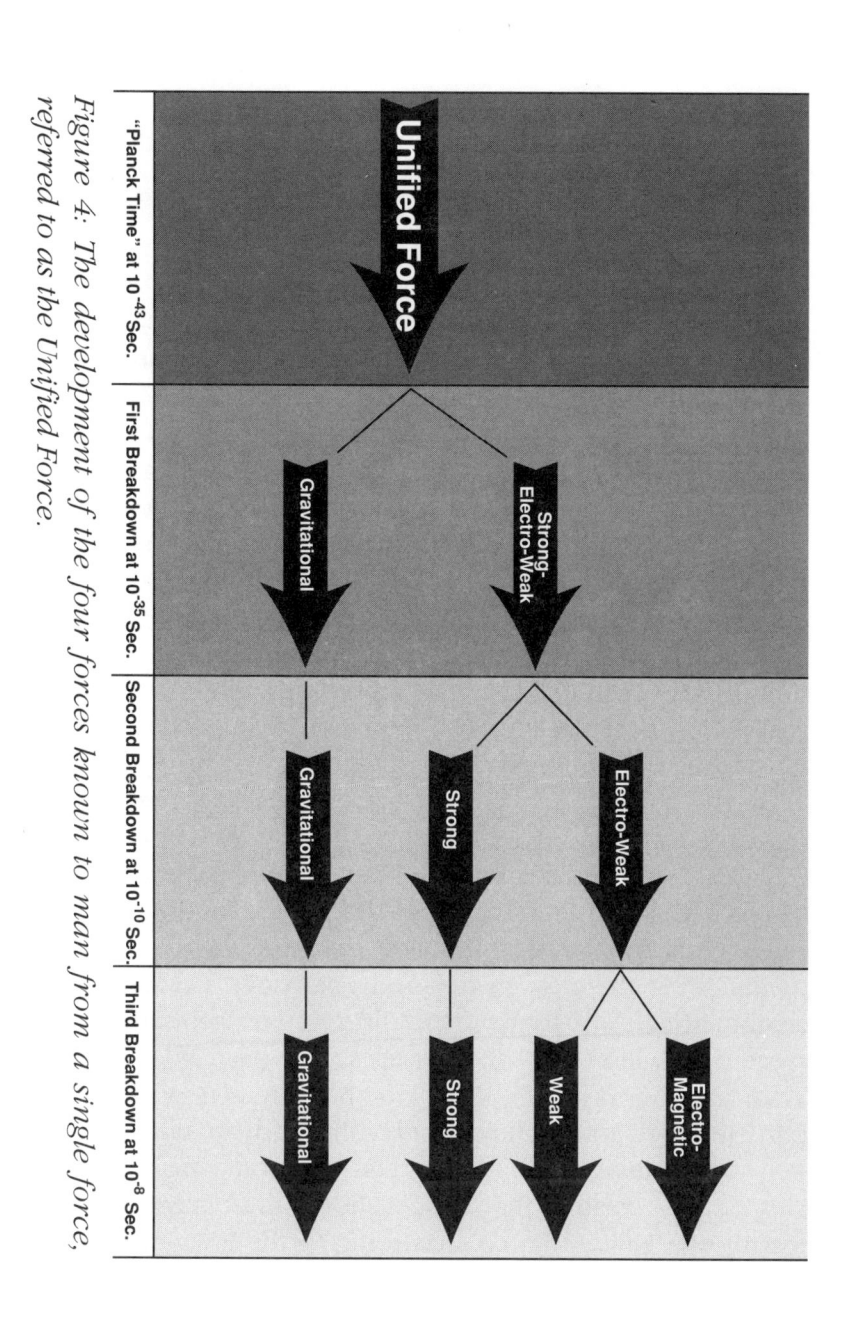

Figure 4: The development of the four forces known to man from a single force, referred to as the Unified Force.

The Inflationary Universe model describes what happened when this single force broke down into four separate forces (see Figure 4). Because we are speculating about time infinitely approaching zero, we need to imagine this process in reverse and consider unification rather than the synthesis of the individual forces. Thus, at 10^{-6} seconds, the protons and neutrons are broken down into quarks, and at 10^{-10} seconds, the first unification takes place between the electromagnetic and weak forces, to form the *electroweak* force. This can be duplicated in laboratory experiments. At this point, there are three major forces: *electroweak, strong,* and *gravitational.* Going back further in time to 10^{-35} seconds, the strong and the electroweak forces unify to form the *strong-electroweak* force. At this point, two main forces exist: *strong-electroweak,* and *gravitational.* This unification cannot be duplicated in laboratory experiments because of the massive amounts of energy required. Going back further in time to 10^{-43} seconds, the final unification between these two main forces takes place. The name given to the time when final unification occurs is *Planck Time.*

According to the laws of quantum mechanics, at *Planck Time,* particles and anti-particles may appear in an excited state of vacuum and destroy each other. This phenomenon is called *quantum fluctuation.* According to the latest theories, matter and antimatter are slightly asymmetrical. So, for every billion or so anti-particles created, a billion and one particles may have been created, and because of the destructive interaction of the particles and anti-particles, only one particle of matter may have survived. If during this time some mass was successfully created, then some energy must have been lost by the Unified Force, according to the laws of conservation of energy. Under certain conditions, this creation of mass could begin and continue for a time. As the creation of mass continues, further energy is drained from the Unified Force until this force breaks down to the *strong-electroweak* and *gravitational.* At this point, the newly created mass undergoes an expansion of a magnitude of 10^{50}.

At such rates of expansion, a small amount of mass could fill the entire Universe. This point can be illustrated with more comprehensible numbers. As an example, if we took one cubic meter of mass and kept doubling it (see Figure 5), notice what would happen to the area of each plane:

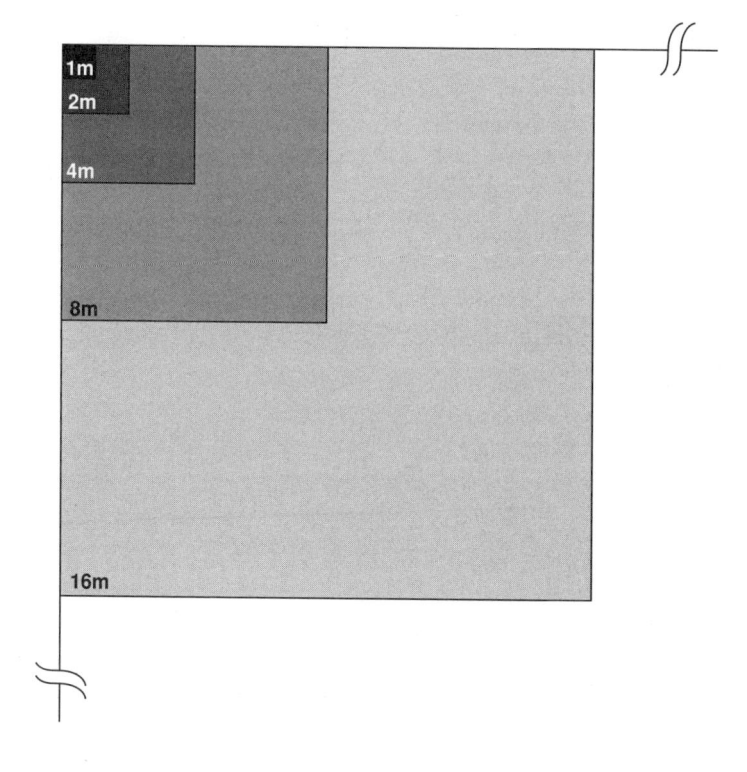

Figure 5: Graphical Illustration of the expansion process

The initial state is 1 meter (2^0)
The 1st result produces 2 meters (2^1)
The 2nd result produces 4 meters (2^2)
The 3rd result produces 8 meters (2^3)
The 4th result produces 16 meters (2^4)
The 5th result produces 32 meters (2^5)
The 6th result produces 64 meters (2^6)
The 7th result produces 128 meters (2^7)
The 8th result produces 256 meters (2^8)
The 9th result produces 512 meters (2^9)
The 10th result produces 1,024 meters (2^{10})
The 11th result produces 2,048 meters (2^{11})
The 12th result produces 4,096 meters (2^{12})
The 13th result produces 8,192 meters (2^{13})
The 14th result produces 16,284 meters (2^{14})

.

.

.

The 50th result produces 1,125,899,060,000,000 meters (2^{50}). This last result is about 6,950 times larger than the distance between the Earth and the Sun (162 million kilometers) in every direction. This example uses base 2. Can you imagine how huge our result would have been if we had used base 10 instead?

As the Universe cools further, the inflationary process stops; however, the momentum of the expansion continues, and the strong force separates from the electroweak force. Finally, the weak force is separated from the electromagnetic force, allowing the protons, neutrons, and electrons to form. Further cooling allows the simple atoms, such as helium and hydrogen, to form cosmic particles. Still further cooling allows the condensation of the cosmic particles to form the stars and planets. Over hundreds of millions of years, all other material is created, to make up the galaxies as we know them.

Even if the Inflationary Universe model is accurate, the question remains: Where did this Unified Force come from? For the quantum fluctuation to occur, an excited vacuum state must be present. How did this excited vacuum come into existence? How far did this vacuum extend? If this phenomenon took place in this universe, is it likely to have happened in other universes?

This leads us to one conclusion: Because there cannot be existence without a beginning, there must be a force beyond the natural laws of the Universe. Such a force controls the Universe yet is not constrained by its laws. Whatever the creative force is, it is powerful enough to have created the Universe and is far beyond our comprehension.

The Universe is just too organized to have occurred randomly. For the Universe to exist according to the Inflationary Universe model, the magnitude of expansion had to have been precise. If the force of expansion had been any smaller, the process would have reversed itself, and the cosmic particles would have collapsed on themselves, reverting to singularity. If the force of expansion had been greater, the cosmic particles would have been too far apart to condense, and galaxies would not have formed.

Since we cannot prove that the Universe created itself, it follows that evolutionary theories claiming that life on Earth of any form was started by accident are also unlikely to be true. If there is a macro level creative force, the same type of force is probably also involved on a micro level. Just look around you and observe the thousands of species, each with its beauty, function, and habitat. Look at the microscopic creatures, the atoms, the plants, and how each is designed in a unique way.

If we use the terminology of Christianity, Judaism, or Islam, this Creative Force, whether on a macro or micro level is called *God* or *Allah*. These are some of the names for the Creative Force; it does not matter which one you use. The implicit belief in this force is the foundation of all major religions. All religions stipulate that this force is "all good," omnipotent, omniscient, omnipresent, and serious about its relationship with us.

Now that we have discussed the Creator, let's consider the Creation. According to the Old Testament, God created the Universe, including Adam and Eve, in six days and rested on the seventh. If you trace Biblical chronology from Adam to the present, you would estimate the Creation to have occurred about 12,000 years ago. This is contrary to what scientific discoveries indicate. Fossils of hard-bodied living creatures date back well over 700,000,000 (700 million) years. We may eventually find older fossils of hard-bodied creatures on Earth. Microfossil traces of single-cell life forms date back as far as 3,500,000,000 (3.5 billion) years. Using radioisotopic dating, the Earth is estimated to have been in existence for 4,550,000,000 (4.5 billion) years.

Is the Bible wrong? Before I attempt to answer this question, a number of issues must be addressed.

Where did life come from?

There are scientists who believe that life on Earth and possibly elsewhere in the Universe may have formed by itself, by accident, that there was no Creator and no predesign. Certain laboratory experiments have been conducted in the hope of producing a living cell, the basic unit of life. In these experiments, the conditions resembling those of our evolving planet about 3,500,000,000

(3.5 billion) years ago were duplicated, and, with the help of electric sparks and other factors, amino acids and proteins were produced. However, all experiments have failed to produce a single living cell.

Other theories claim that life on Earth may have come from other parts of the Universe, carried here by meteorites or comet fragments. Such theories, however, are just theories. There is no firm proof of their truth. Even if these theories are accurate, how did life exist aboard a meteorite or comet? How did it survive entry into Earth's atmosphere? Where did it come from? And how did such life produce the complex structures of living creatures on Earth?

How long did it take to create the Universe?

When we are told that the Universe was created in six days, are we talking about Earth days? Remember that each Earth day represents a complete 360 degree rotation of the planet. Just as the Earth and other planets of the Solar System rotate around the Sun once a year, an Earth year is longer than a year on Mercury and considerably shorter than a year on Jupiter or Saturn. The Sun rotates around the Milky Way galaxy once every 230,000,000 (230 Million) Earth years (one Sun year). As you can see, time is a relative measurement, and without further clarification of the six-day creation reference point, we have no idea what a God's day represents.

What is the origin of evil?

"**And out of the ground made the Lord God to grow every tree that is pleasant to the sight, and good for food; the tree of life also in the midst of the garden, and the tree of knowledge of good and**

17

evil." (Genesis 2:9). This clearly indicates that evil was in existence before the fall of Adam and Eve. If God is "all good" and is the sole Creator, why did evil come into existence? Why doesn't Genesis mention anything about it? Some theories propose that evil may have come into existence after a group of angels rebelled against God and were transformed from good into evil beings. In reality, no one knows.

What is even more puzzling is this passage from the Old Testament: **"Now there was a day when the sons of God came to present themselves before the Lord, and Satan came also among them." (Job 1:6).** Does Satan have the power to appear in any place he pleases? What kind of powers does Satan possess? Why is there contact between good and evil in this passage, given that they are conflicting forces? If you read **Job 1:7-12**, you will detect no sign of a clash between God and Satan, and, as a matter of fact, if what was written is true, they communicated dispassionately and logically.

If Adam was created by a power who is "all good," why was it necessary to test Adam's goodness? Just as we have accepted the premise that there is a Creator who is "all good," we now have to accept the premise that there is an opposing force of unknown origin that is "all evil" and that every creature in the Universe has to be subjected to the powers of these two forces. It seems that no human being has ever been able to escape this conflict between good and evil. Even Christ and the other prophets of God were put to the test.

But what does this mean? What are the consequences of choosing evil? According to the Bible: **"but of the fruit of the tree which is in the midst of the garden, God hath said, Ye shall not eat of it, neither shall ye** touch it, lest ye die." (Genesis 3:3). So if Adam and Eve had not eaten from this tree, they might have lived forever. Instead, because they ate the fruit, they were condemned to die: **"in the sweat of thy face shalt thou eat bread, till thou return unto the ground; for out of it wast thou taken: for dust thou art, and unto dust shalt thou return." (Genesis 3:19).** Was it really a serpent that tempted Eve? Did Adam and Eve communicate with all animals, or was the serpent another symbol for Satan?

Was the Forbidden Fruit Just a Fruit?

Doesn't it seem odd to condemn Adam and Eve to die for eating a forbidden fruit? Or is this fruit really a symbol for something else, such as sex? If they were not meant to have sex, why were Adam and Eve created with reproductive organs? Were they created with reproductive organs just in case they failed the test? Or did God know that they would fail the test? Or were they really not the first human-like creatures? Prior to the fall of Adam and Eve, who was Adam addressing when he said **"Therefore shall a man leave his father and his mother, and shall cleave unto his wife: and they shall be one flesh." (Genesis 2:24).** Was this a prophecy that sexual intercourse would produce children? Isn't it strange to hear such words from a fatherless and motherless creature?

Was the Garden of Eden on Earth?

According to the Bible: **"So he drove out the man: and he placed at the east of the garden of Eden cherubim, and a flaming sword which turned every way, to keep the way of the tree of life." (Genesis 3:24).** If it really is on Earth, why has no one ever seen the cherubim and the flaming sword? In the Koran: **"Then did Satan make them slip from the (Garden), and get them out of the state (of felicity) in which they had been. We said: 'Get ye down, all (ye people), with enmity between yourselves. On earth will be your dwelling-place and your means of livelihood for a time.' " (Sura II: Baqara 36).** "Get ye down" is the English translation of the Arabic word that means "to descend." But to descend from where? Also "on earth will be your dwelling..." indicates their dwelling place must previously have been somewhere else.

How did the descendants of Adam populate the Earth?

When Adam and Eve were driven out of the Garden of Eden, they had two sons, Cain and Abel. When Cain killed Abel: **"...And the Lord set a mark upon Cain, lest any finding him should kill him." (Genesis 4:15).** Who was there besides Adam and Eve to kill him? Adam was 130 years old when his third son Seth was born.

Now, consider this passage: **"And Cain knew his wife; and she conceived, and bare Enoch: and he builded a city, and called the name of the city, after the name of his son, Enoch." (Genesis 4:17).** But where did Cain's wife come from? Also, why was Cain building a city? How many inhabitants of Earth were there to justify building a city? And here is another passage: **"There were giants in the earth in those days; and also after that, when the sons of God came in unto the daughters of men, and they bare children to them, the same became mighty men which were of old, men of renown." (Genesis 6:4).** Who were these giants? If the male descendants of Adam were known as the "sons of God," why were the daughters called "daughters of men," unless they were not Adam's descendants? All indications lead me to believe that the Earth was already inhabited by human beings when Adam and Eve descended from the Garden of Eden (wherever it was).

This brings me back to the question posed earlier: Is the Bible wrong, or is our scientific data wrong? I believe that they are both correct. Theologians are correct in saying that Adam lived and fathered his first descendants some 12,000 years ago, but they are incorrect in linking the presence of Adam and Eve to the beginning of life on Earth. The Earth has gone through billions of years of development and has always supported some form of life.

Just as Adam was not the first life form on Earth, neither is the Earth the only place in the Universe where life exists. Actually, if you were to compare Earth to the rest of the Universe, you would realize that it is no more than a speck of dust. If you were to use mathematical probabilities to determine how many Earth-like planets exist in the Universe and may support life, you would be shocked. Even if you were able to find only one similar planet in each galaxy, each containing billions of stars, you would find millions of similar planets, since there are millions of galaxies.

But who said that life elsewhere in the Universe has to exist in the form of human flesh and blood? Let's face it, God would not go to the trouble of creating a universe so vast just so we could admire the starlight at night. There was a purpose in creating the Universe, just as there was a purpose in creating every species. **"We cre-**

ated not the heavens, the earth, and all between them, merely in (idle) sport: We created them not except for just ends: But most of them do not understand." (Sura XLIV: Dukhãn 38-39). But how does it all tie together? Since science is unable to produce an explanation, we must attempt to find such answers by examining religious beliefs.

CHAPTER 2

RELIGIONS

Nothing is more distressing than seeing the way religions are practiced today. People from all walks of life follow religious sects as if blindfolded, while others have turned away from religion to Atheism because some of the things they have heard or read make no sense. Still others have turned to cults because they offer another way of life or alternative explanations to those of traditional religions. The formation of cults has, in some cases, lead to disasters, such as the Jim Jones tragedy in Guyana. Christianity is now subdivided into hundreds of sects; Islam and Judaism are also subdivided. Every sect claims to be "correct." How can we determine who is right and who is wrong? Unfortunately, people have forgotten the very essence of religions: *seeking the truth about our existence and our relationship with the Creator.*

But how can you seek the truth if you are raised not to question what your priest or religious leaders tell you? If you are a Christian, please read the New Testament and try to analyze what it says. If you are a Moslem, please read and analyze the Koran. If you are a Jew, read and analyze the Old Testament. A true intellectual will not take things for granted but will research the subject matter for as long as necessary to form an opinion.

No matter which religion you belong to or which Holy Book you believe in, the underlying essence of all religions is the same. All religions call for

- The belief in one Creator, no matter whether you call this Creating Force God, Allah, or some other name
- Decent and righteous human behavior
- The belief in life after death

Since the essence of all religions is the same, does it really matter how you worship your Creator? Does it really matter which church, mosque, or synagogue you attend, which food you eat, or whether you face Mecca when you pray?

It is very important to separate the essence of a religion from the social application of that religion. A religion comes into existence at a certain time and in a certain place for a certain group of people. It develops in a form these people can accept, at their level of comprehension. Islam, for example, came to the people of the Arabian Peninsula in a form that was consistent with their life-style and understanding. The only way at that time to spread Islam was through the power of the sword. Tribes imposed their way of living on other tribes only by force. Islam couldn't have come to the people of this region with the message "Love thy neighbor."

As a religion evolves, its essence is accompanied by a set of practices developed by its founder and later by its followers. Thus, religious holidays come into existence to mark significant events, prayer evolves in a form that cannot easily be forgotten, and specific rules develop to govern marriage, death, health, and other aspects of life.

Jews today are following the same social customs of their religion that have been practiced since Moses; Christians, since Christ; and Moslems, since Mohammed.

Even the youngest of these three religions is about 1400 years old. Isn't it about time that people looked at traditional laws and questioned how applicable they are to life in the twentieth century? Does it make sense to incite a religious revolution to force the people of the twentieth century to adhere strictly to rules that were first imposed on the people of the sixth century? Is the emergence of Islamic Fundamentalism or far-right Jewish Fundamentalism a positive direction for this era?

Some religions develop to complement older religions. Christianity was one of these. **"...an eye for an eye, and a tooth for a tooth" (Leviticus 24:20)** from Judaism is replaced in Christianity by **"...whosoever shall smite thee on thy right cheek, turn to him the other also." (Matthew 5:38-39).** In the First Century, Jews were ready to shake loose the social rules and regulations that they had inherited a few thousand years earlier and move on to a more mature level. Christ challenged these social rules without contradicting the Ten Commandments.

This is illustrated in several Biblical passages when Christ violated the traditions of the Sabbath. **"And he said unto them, The Sabbath was made for man, and not man for the Sabbath." (Mark 2:27).** **"He answered and said unto them, Well hath Isaiah prophesied of you hypocrites, as it is written, This people honoreth me with their lips, but their heart is far from me. Howbeit in vain do they worship me, teaching for doctrines the commandments of men. For laying aside the commandments of God,** ye hold the tradition of men, as the washing of pots and cups: and many other such like things ye do." (Mark 7:6-8). "Think not that I am come to destroy the law, or the prophets: I am not come to destroy, but to fulfil." (Matthew 5:17).

Islam, on the other hand, came to Atheist nations, and in no way does it reject Judaism or Christianity. As a matter of fact, Jews and Christians were not forced to convert during the Islamic expansion. **"Those who believe (in the Koran), and those who follow the Jewish (scriptures), and the Christians and the Sabians, any who believe in God and the Last Day, and work righteousness, shall have their reward with their Lord: on them shall be no fear, nor shall they grieve." (Sura II: Baqara 62).** Islam explains some of the mysteries that are mentioned in the Bible but unfortunately creates some of its own.

Since the essence of all religions is the same, any individual who seeks to broaden his understanding of religions should feel free to study all Holy Books, stripping away the social aspects of each and then comparing them without bias.

Keep in mind, however, that the accuracy of all Holy Books is in question. There is no denying that many of the events mentioned did take place; however, certain details have been added; others, deleted. The various pieces of the New Testament, for example, were not collected into one volume for hundreds of years after Christ. Similarly, the Koran was memorized and recited before it was written down. Isn't it likely that error was introduced in the process? Just like the Bible, the Koran wasn't compiled in a single volume for a long time after Mohammed.

The original messages of most religions, then, had probably been altered through repeated recitation before they were written down. As these writings were compiled, essential material may have been lost, and nonessential material may have been added. And as any Holy Book was translated into other languages, further error may have been introduced. Improperly chosen words may have had a significant effect on meaning.

It is extremely painful to hear of a war or a regional conflict that is fueled by religious hatred. History has given us many examples of such conflicts. There were the Christian Crusades of the eleventh through the thirteenth centuries, which attempted to free the Holy Land from the hands of the Moslems. And there have been many such wars in modern times: the wars between the Arabs and Israel, the civil wars in Cyprus, Lebanon, and Ireland, and the conflict in India between Sïkh and Hindu and between Moslem and Hindu. Such conflicts are actually economic or territorial, with a religious facade. Why is it that some members of one religion look down on those of another? How can such people be absolutely sure that they are right and that others are wrong? What role do religious leaders play in fueling such behavior?

If you travel by car from Jeddah to Taïf in Saudi Arabia, you reach a point where the road is closed to everyone but Moslems because it passes through Mecca. People of other faiths must take a long detour, commonly called "the Road of the Infidels." Are the Moslems of Saudi Arabia following the true spirit of Mohammed's message? What makes these Moslems think they are pure but other people are unclean?

It is time for such barriers to be removed. Unlike political barriers, such as the Berlin Wall, which lasted for only a few decades, the barriers of religious hatred and discrimination have endured for centuries. How can fathers and mothers raise their children to look down — even hate— those of other faiths? How can such hatred be reversed? Can the people of Lebanon heal their wounds overnight? Is a son able to forgive the opposing group for killing his father? The American Civil War ended over a century ago, yet racial hatred and discrimination still persist in the hearts of some Americans. Religious civil wars have the same consequences.

Truly rational people, rather than adopt the hatred fostered by religious wars, first try to understand what their own religion teaches, then what the "opposing" religion teaches. But the ultimate force to change, to bring an end to hatred, can only come from within and through a better understanding of the mysteries of life and death.

CHAPTER 3

LIFE AND DEATH

Do you recall anything about the period prior to your birth? Do you know for certain what awaits you after you die? The answer to these two questions is nowhere to be found in scientific or religious textbooks. No one can claim this knowledge except God. The only thing we can do is study available information on the subject and then draw conclusions.

A child is born in sub-Saharan Africa. There is a good chance that this child may not even live to be an adult. Diseases, poverty, and famine may make this child's life a painful experience. At that same instant, a child is born to a middle class family in the United States, where medicine is available, food is plentiful, and the elements of civilized living are in place. Compare the two cases and ask yourself the following question: Is it really fair to have such wide diversities in creation? If you believe in "nothingness" prior to your birth, your answer is likely to be no.

Suppose you and I are of the same age, school, class, grade, and background and our school teacher comes to give us a test. For the sake of fairness, the teacher should give the same test to both of us. What if this teacher gives me a 4th grade test but gives you a test appropriate for the 10th grade level? Would you consider this fair? If God is just and fair, why are we born different? All Holy Books call for belief in God and for living by the laws set forth in Holy Scriptures to lead us into a life of eternal happiness after death. But why are we not all subjected to the same conditions on Earth? Why is one person born blind but another born with sight? Why do some people have a harder life than others? Why are some people, such as Einstein or Mozart, born with exceptional talents, yet others are born with few or are even retarded?

The Bible suggests what the reasons for this inequality may be: **"And as Jesus passed by, he saw a man which was blind from his birth. And his disciples asked him, saying, Master, who did sin, this man, or his parents, that he was born blind?" (John 9:1-2).** In other words, there is an association between "sins" and "physical defects." But how could this man be paying for his sins if he was born blind? For this to be true, there must have been a previous life. Another example reinforces this idea: **"And Jesus answered and said unto them, Elijah truly shall first come, and restore all things. But I say unto you, That Elijah is come already, and they knew him not, but have done unto him whatsoever they listed. Likewise shall also the Son of man suffer of them. Then the disciples understood that he spake unto them of John the Baptist." (Matthew 17:11-13).** How could Elijah be John the Baptist? Doesn't this imply that there is a previous life and an after life, in other words, reincarnation?

"The Lord possessed me in the beginning of his way, before his works of old. I was set up from everlasting, from the beginning, or ever the earth was. When there were no depths, I was brought

forth; when there were no fountains abounding with water. Before the mountains were settled, before the hills was I brought forth: While as yet he had not made the earth, nor the fields, nor the highest part of the dust of the world. When he prepared the heavens, I was there: when he set a compass upon the face of the depth: When he established the clouds above: when he strengthened the fountains of the deep: when he gave to the sea his decree, that the waters should not pass his commandment: when he appointed the foundations of the earth: then I was by him, as one brought up with him: and I was daily his delight, rejoicing always before him; Rejoicing in the habitable part of his earth; and my delights were with the sons of men." (Proverbs 8:22-31).** How could Solomon claim to have been with God when he created the Universe unless he truly was there?

Consider the following from the Koran: **"How can ye reject the faith in God? Seeing that ye were without life, and He gave you life; then will He cause you to die, and will again bring you to life; and again to Him will ye return." (Sura II: Baqara 28).** How many times have you felt that you have been to a certain place, but this is your first time there? You may see a person for the first time and feel like you have known this person for years as if he or she is your lost brother or sister, and joy fills your heart. Toward another person, you may feel indifferent; toward another, you may feel hatred for no reason at all. —Or perhaps there is a reason. Your feelings may be the result of an encounter in a previous life.

How many times during a very deep sleep have you "recalled" people you have never known, cities you have never visited, social behavior that is foreign to you? Some of these dreams are quite pleasant, and in many cases, after you wake up, you may wish that you had remained asleep. On the other hand, some of the dreams that occur in deep sleep are horrifying. During a nightmare, you may feel fear you have never felt before, and you may thank God when you awaken that it was just a dream. But was it just a dream? Why do some people have many nightmares, while others have them only rarely?

Whatever we do in this life affects the next life —or, possibly, the next several lives —and whatever we did in the past life affects this life and possibly subsequent lives. Whatever you plant, you harvest. **"Whatever misfortune happens to you, is because of the things your hands have wrought, and for many (of them) He grants forgiveness." (Sura XLII: Shura 30). "Such are the men whom God has cursed for He has made them deaf and blinded their sight." (Sura XLVII: Muhammad 23). "...great in counsel, and mighty in work: for thine eyes are open upon all the ways of the sons of men, to give every one according to his ways, and according to the fruit of his doings..." (Jeremiah 32:19). "The Lord rewarded me according to my righteousness; according to the cleanness of my hands hath he recompensed me." (Psalms 18:20).** This changes the entire picture of fairness. Now we understand that the child of sub-Saharan Africa "deserved" to be born there for reasons only the Almighty knows. This doesn't mean, however, that we shouldn't lend a helping hand.

The common belief that as long as we sincerely ask for forgiveness, we will go to Heaven is improbable. Imagine a person who lives his entire life fearing God and doing nothing but good. Yet another person lives his life in sin, practicing sexual promiscuity and committing all sorts of crimes, from theft to murder. Even if this sinner repents just before death, would it be fair for both the sinner and the saint to be treated equally after death? What incentive do we have to live a righteous life if we can do everything that is forbidden and then "repent" just before we die? Is everything we have done forgiven in this case? Actually, if each individual received full punishment in this life for his or her transgressions, life would be a living hell. But because God is merciful, we in many cases do not receive our punishment to its fullest, but not all our transgressions are entirely forgiven. **"... and that he would show thee the secrets of wisdom, that they are double to that which is! Know therefore that God exacteth of thee less than thine iniquity deserveth." (Job 11:6).**

"Not equal are those believers who sit (at home) and receive no hurt, and those who strive and fight in the cause of God with their goods and their persons. God hath granted a *grade higher* to those who strive and fight with their goods and persons than to those who sit (at home). Unto all (in Faith) hath God promised good: But those who strive and fight hath He distinguished above those who sit (at home) by a special reward, —Ranks specially bestowed by Him and Forgiveness and Mercy. For God is often forgiving, Most Merciful." (Sura IV: Nisãa 95-96). If there are ranks specially bestowed for those who strive in their life over those who do not, there must be a difference between a person who lives his or her entire life righteously compared to a person who lives his or her life in sin and then repents right before he or she dies.

If there is a universal system in place, why wasn't it explained fully in the Holy Books? Is it possible that people were not capable of comprehending such a universal system when the Holy Books were written? Christ used parables to explain certain things, but even so, people had problems understanding: **"Then answered Peter and said unto him, Declare unto us this parable. And Jesus said, Are ye also yet without understanding?" (Matthew 15:15-16). "And he said unto them, Know ye not this parable? and how then will ye know all parables?" (Mark 4:13). "But without a parable spake he not unto them: and when they were alone, he expounded all things to his disciples." (Mark 4:34). "If I have told you earthly things, and ye believe not, how shall ye believe, if I tell you of heavenly things?" (John 3:12).**

The Bible and the Koran talk about Heaven and Hell as two poles (see Figure 6). Some religious sects such as Catholicism have introduced "limbo" or nothingness for non-Catholics. It is believed that non-Catholics will enter into a state of eternal "unsatisfied longing" as their only torment because they will not be exposed to the sight of God. This is one of the most negative beliefs in Catholic doctrine. How could Catholics believe that every non-Catholic is doomed? On the other hand, Catholicism correctly identifies Heaven and Hell as being broken down into different levels, but Catholics incorrectly attempt to place certain people (such as saints or priests) in the different layers of heaven as if they have been there. These levels could better be understood by reading Dante's Paradiso and Inferno or other books on Catholicism.

In reality, we are living in a place where flashes of suffering and happiness are combined at various levels to form our life. In other words, we are at times in a

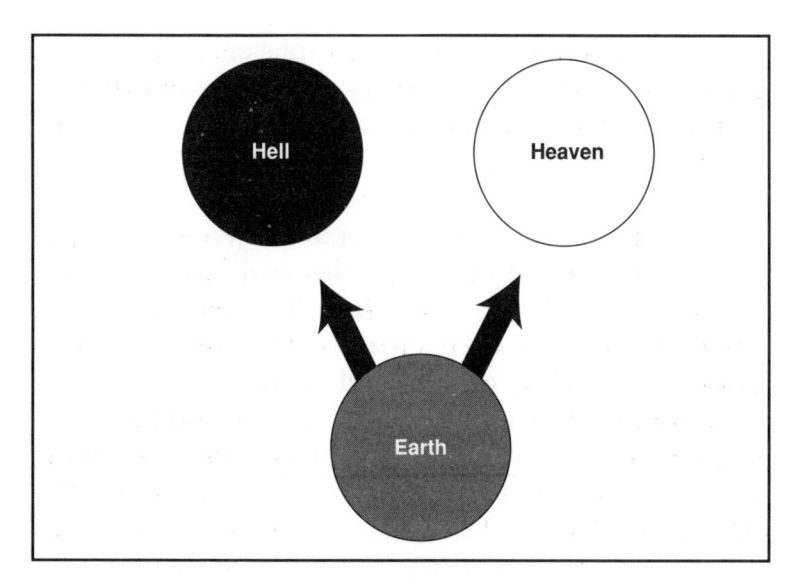

Figure 6: It is commonly believed that, after death, man will go either to Heaven or Hell.

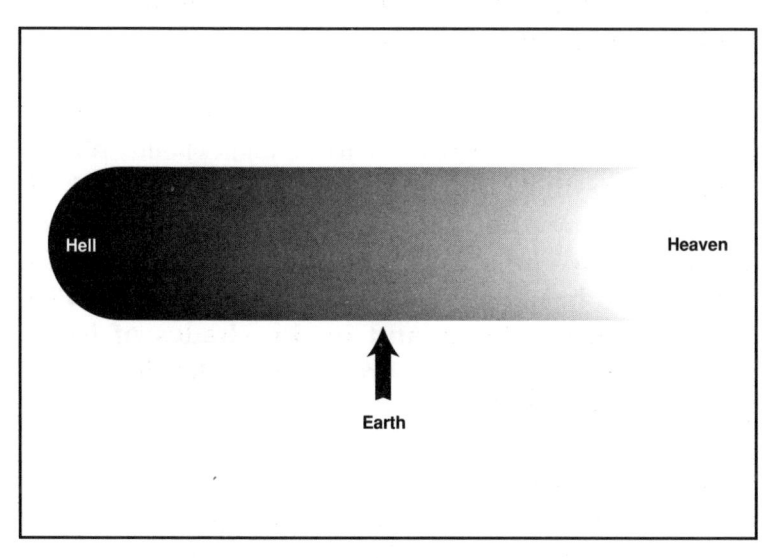

Figure 7: After every life cycle, depending on our deeds, we may fall anywhere in the spectrum.

hell-like environment and at other times in a heaven-like environment. The extreme poles of Heaven and Hell are now connected by a spectrum of a certain breadth (see Figure 7).

It is impossible to move from any reference point to absolute Heaven in one step. This requires perfection, and who is perfect? **"And when he was gone forth into the way, there came one running, and kneeled to him, and asked him, Good Master, what shall I do that I may inherit eternal life? And Jesus said unto him, Why callest thou me good? there is none good but one, that is, God." (Mark 10:17-18).** (Based on this, anyone who claims that Jesus is God is a hypocrite.) An immediate leap into Heaven might require tests of love, loyalty, and other qualities beyond our comprehension. **"And no man hath ascended up to heaven, but he that came down from heaven, even the Son of man which is in heaven." (John 3:13).**

The same is true of Hell, where multiple reincarnation cycles prevent the regression to absolute hell: **"Where their worm dieth not, and the fire is not quenched. For every one shall be salted with fire, and every sacrifice shall be salted with salt." (Mark 9:48-49). "(They will be) in the midst of a fierce Blast of Fire and in Boiling Water, and in the shades of Black Smoke: Nothing (will there be) to refresh, nor to please..." (Sura LVI: Wãqi'a 42-44).**

For every evil thing we do, punishment awaits us, either in this life or the next. We must pay for every sin that we commit. On the other hand, we will be repaid for every good and righteous thing.

It is important to keep in mind that we are no longer talking about a system which applies only to life on Earth but a system that encompasses life in a universe with billions of stars in each galaxy. We now understand what was meant by **"In my father's house are many mansions..." (John 14:2)** and by **"There is one glory of the sun, and another glory of the moon, and another glory of the stars; for one star differeth from another star in glory." (1 Corinthians 15:41).**

When we refer to life, we are not necessarily talking about life in a human form. Each world has its own rules and regulations that govern the lives of its inhabitants. Furthermore, we are no longer talking only about the human species but rather about all living species. Animals, plants, and inanimate matter are also part of this universe. They have emotions and the freedom to choose between good and evil.

You may have been an animal, plant, or an inanimate object in a previous life, and it is quite possible that you may take on such a life in the future.

Animals, although they cannot speak, have a world of their own with certain rules governing it. They have to choose between good and evil just as we do. The problem is that, for a purpose unknown to us, we cannot communicate with them. **"There is not an animal (that lives) on the earth, nor a being that flies on its wings, but (forms part of) communities like you. Nothing have we omitted from the Book, and they (all) shall be gathered to their Lord in the end." (Sura VI: An'âm 38).** "But ask now the beasts, and they shall teach thee: and the fowls of the air, and they shall tell thee: or speak to the earth, and it shall teach thee; and the fishes of the sea shall delare unto thee. Who knoweth not in all these that the hand of the Lord hath wrought this? In whose hand is the soul of every living thing, and the breath of all mankind." (Job 12:7-10).** So when we deal with an animal, we should really treat it just the way we treat any other soul.

"And the ass saw the angel of the Lord standing in the way, and his sword drawn in his hand: and the ass turned aside out of the way, and went into the field: and Balaam smote the ass, to turn her into the way. But the angel of the Lord stood in a path of the vineyards, a wall being on this side, and a wall on that side. And when the ass saw the angel of the Lord, she thrust herself unto the wall, and crushed Balaam's foot against the wall: and he smote her again. And the angel of the Lord went further, and stood in a narrow place, where was no way to turn either to the right hand or to the left. And when the ass saw the angel of the Lord, she fell down under Balaam: and Balaam's anger was kindled, and he smote the ass with a staff. And the Lord opened the mouth of the ass, and she said unto Balaam, What have I done unto thee, that thou hast smitten me these three times? And Balaam said unto the ass, Because thou hast mocked me: I would there were a sword in mine hand, for now would I kill thee. And the ass said unto Balaam, Am not I thine ass, upon which thou hast ridden ever since I was thine unto this day? Was I ever wont to do so unto thee? And he said, Nay. Then the Lord opened the eyes of Balaam, and he saw the angel of the Lord standing in the way, and his sword in his hand: and he bowed down his head, and fell flat on his face. And the angel of the Lord said unto him, Wherefore hast thou smitten thine ass these three times? Behold, I went out to withstand thee, because thy way is perverse before me: and the ass saw me, and turned from me these three times: unless she had turned from me, surely now also I had slain thee, and saved her alive." (Numbers 22:23-33).

This passage is taken from the Koran: **"And before Solomon were marshalled His hosts, —of Jinns and men and birds, and they were all kept in order and ranks. At length, when they came to a (lowly) valley of ants, One of the ants said: 'O ye ants, get into your habitations, lest Solomon and his hosts crush you (under foot) without knowing it.' So he smiled, amused at her speech; and he said: 'O my Lord! so order me that I may be grateful for thy favours, which thou hast bestowed on me and on my parents, and that I may work the righteousness that will please Thy Grace, to the ranks of Thy Righteous Servants.' "** (Sura XXVII: Naml 17-19).

"Seest thou not that it is God Whose praises all beings in the heavens and on earth do celebrate, and the birds (of the air) with wings outspread? Each one knows its own (mode of) prayer and praise. And God knows well all that they do." (Sura XXIV: Nur 41). "And the herbs and the trees —both (alike) bow in adoration." (Sura LV: Rahmān 6). "We have decreed Death to be your common lot, and we are not to be frustrated from changing your Forms and creating you (again) in (Forms) that ye know not." (Sura LVI: Wāqi'a 60-61).

"Say: 'Shall I point out to you something much worse than this, (as judged) by the treatment it received from God? Those who incurred the curse of God and His wrath, those of whom some he transformed into apes and swine, Those who worshiped Evil; —These are (many times) worse in rank, and far more astray from the even Path!' " (Sura V: Mãida 63).

"They say : 'What! When we are reduced to bones and dust, should we really be raised up (to be) a new creation?' Say: '(Nay!) be ye stones or iron, or created matter which, in your minds, is hardest (to be raised up)! —(yet shall ye be raised up)!'..." (Sura XVII: Bani Isrã'il 49-51).

The cycle of reincarnation continues as long as a single sin is committed. Now we understand what was meant by **"For the wages of sin is death..." (Romans 6-23)** or by **"Marvel not that I said unto thee, Ye must be born again." (John 3:7).** Once we are sinless, eternal life awaits us, and death is no more. On the other hand, if we continue to regress, eternal suffering is our destination. From this viewpoint, when we look around us and see the healthy and the sick, the wealthy and the poor, the talented and the ignorant, we realize that we are governed by a just and universal system. **"Those who reject our signs are deaf and dumb, —in the midst of darkness profound: whom God willeth, he leaveth to wander: whom He willeth, He placeth on the Way that is Straight." (Sura VI: An'ãm`39).**

Life may not necessarily be serial, for there could be parts of us living at the same time in this world or any other world or worlds. The link between life forms in the Universe is accomplished through spiritual fluids. Spiritual fluids are the extension of the spirit to the animate or inanimate world, and once the last spiritual fluid is directed away from a particular life form, the phenomenon called death takes place.

As an example of a spiritual link, suppose that an individual is involved in a very noble cause. This action may trigger what is called a "spiritual fluid" to leave this individual and be directed toward another place in the Universe, where it takes on a certain form of life, and where the conditions are much nicer as a reward for this good deed. At this point in the concurrent life of this individual, a different life experience occurs, and the choice between good and evil takes place at a different level. The spiritual fluid is linked to the individual on Earth like a vector. In reality, our life is nothing but a collection of spiritual fluids being directed from this world toward other worlds, directed from other worlds toward this world, directed between two or more worlds, or directed from this world into another point or other points in this world. —It may even be a combination of all these things. The same thing holds true if an evil act is committed (see Figure 8).

Such links explain the advancement of this civilization, for certain links to higher worlds produce people like Einstein, Mozart, Beethoven, Michelangelo, and Shakespeare. Similarly, links to the lower worlds produce people like Rasputin, Charles Manson, and Judas Iscariot. Spiritual fluids, whether good or bad, can also be acquired through contact with other people. It is for this specific reason that prolonged exposure to evil groups tends to have a negative impact on us, while exposure to righteous groups tends to have a positive impact.

The effects of sexual behavior are even more pronounced. Individuals involved in a sexual relationship can share or exchange certain spiritual fluids that may

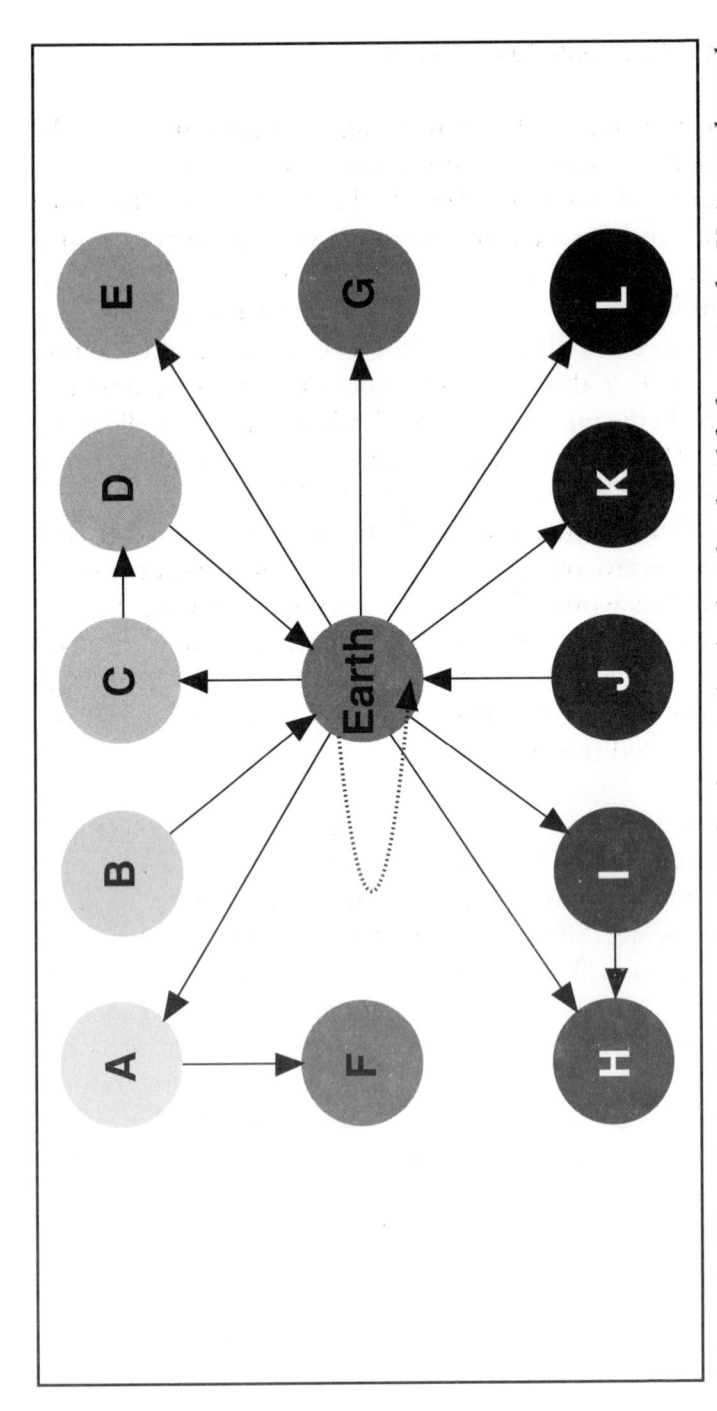

Figure 8: A hypothetical link between the life of an individual with other life forms in the Universe through "spiritual fluids." Darker colors denote worse worlds; lighter colors, better worlds.

link them to each other in this world or to a lower world for many lives to come, thus hindering their spiritual progression toward a better world. For this reason, promiscuous sexual behavior is forbidden in all religions, although traditional religion does not explain why.

We should not look at death as a bad thing but rather as a new beginning. As long as the individual lives his or her life righteously, there is nothing to worry about. If the deceased person did not lead a righteous existence, may God have mercy on him or her, for the suffering he or she undergoes in the next life may be extreme. **"Afterward Jesus findeth him in the temple, and said unto him, Behold, thou art made whole: Sin no more, lest a worse thing come unto thee." (John 9:14).**

One important aspect of reincarnation is that no one, except God and his prophets, knows anything about his or her previous life, so that we can choose between good and evil freely, and not out of fear. Can you imagine living your life knowing that in a previous life you had killed someone? If the same situation occurs again, will you refrain from killing because you remember the punishment you received for your action in a past life, or will you refrain because you want good to triumph over evil? If any individual claims the knowledge of your past life or lives, without solid proof that he or she is a prophet sent by God, you should not believe these claims.

CHAPTER 4

CAUSE AND EFFECT, LIFE'S REALITIES AND AMBIGUITIES

Many of the things in life that we take for granted are not as simple as we might think. For example, what could be simpler than rain itself? Rain replenishes our wells, waters the land so that vegetation can grow, provides drinking water for all creatures, cleans the air from pollutants, and provides ample water for washing our clothes and cars and for bathing. Sometimes, too much rain falls in a certain area and causes flooding, damage to property, loss of life, and hardship. People call this an act of nature and bad luck, but why did this act of nature target a certain geographical area? Why would a tornado hit a certain town? Is it luck? **"Seest thou not that God makes the clouds move gently, then joins them together, then makes them into a heap? —Then wilt thou see rain issue forth from their midst. And He sends down from the sky mountain masses (of clouds) wherein is hail: He strikes therewith whom He pleases and He turns it away from whom He pleases. The vivid flash of His lightning well-nigh blinds the sight." (Sura XXIV: Nur 43).**

If you believe that such a violent act of nature is nothing but a random occurrence, think again. These occurrences are no more random than Noah's flood. There exists a system of cause and effect that, although we cannot directly observe it, governs the world we live in. Nothing meaningful happens randomly or without a reason. "Luck" does not exist. When you are gambling and toss a pair of dice, the outcome is purely statistical. If you happen to roll a pair of 6's, it is because you had a chance of one in 36 (6 x 6) of rolling them. Incidents like this are not meaningful and serve no purpose.

On the other hand, suppose while reading a book, you suddenly get an urge to go to the supermarket and pick up some milk. As you are driving to the store, another car comes out of nowhere, runs a stop sign, and slams into your car, severely injuring its driver but leaving you unharmed. Is this incident a random occurrence, or was it meant to happen? The other driver swears that he didn't see the stop sign. What made you leave at that particular time? Why did this "accident" take place?

An earthquake may hit a city and cause major damage to most buildings; some may even collapse. Immediately, rescue teams spring into action and work around the clock to find survivors. After days of being buried under the rubble, one individual is rescued, but all other members of his family are found dead. Is this luck? Why did the earthquake hit this particular city in the first place? Why are some people devastated, while others are not harmed at all? Why does the man survive but the rest of his family die? Why does this survivor sustain so much pain and suffering? **"No misfortune can happen on earth or in your souls but is recorded in a decree before We bring it into existence: That is truly easy for God..." (Sura LVII: Hadid 22).**

An airline passenger decides at the last minute to

change his flight plans. Later, he hears on the news that a passenger plane has crashed and killed all passengers. To his shock, it is the flight that he was supposed to have taken. What made him alter his travel schedule at that moment? Was it a stroke of luck that he missed the flight, or was it somehow "pre-arranged?" Another plane crashes, and only a handful of passengers survive. Why do these particular passengers survive and not the others?

Why do accidents happen? Are they what we think they are, or are they carefully executed arrangements? You may have heard this phrase in physics that describes the behavior of forces: "For every action, there is an equal and opposite reaction." In the just universal system that we live under, the same principle applies, but the phrase used to describe it is "cause and effect." That is, for every cause, there is an equal effect. Such an effect may be either positive or negative. If you inflict pain on another individual, pain will be inflicted on you. If you cheat and steal, you will be cheated and stolen from. On the other hand, if you live righteously and do nothing but good, the effect will be positive, and you will be rewarded in this life or in the life or lives to come. Such negative and positive reactions summarize what happens to us in real life. Even if it takes tens of incarnations to happen, there will be a reaction to each of your actions. It is quite possible that the results of your actions will occur not only in this world but in other worlds as well. **"(Remember also) Qarun, Pharaoh, and Haman: there came to them Moses with Clear Signs, but they behaved with insolence on the earth; yet they could not overreach (Us).** *Each one of them We seized for his crime:* **of them against some We sent a violent tornado (with showers of stones); some were caught by a (mighty) Blast; some We caused the**

Earth to swallow up; and some We drowned (in the waters): It was not God Who injured (or oppressed) them: They injured (and oppressed) their own souls." (Sura XXIX: Ankabut 39-40).

This is where the big blur comes: If Christ's teachings replaced the maxim "an eye for an eye, and a tooth for a tooth" with **"...whosoever shall smite thee on thy right cheek, turn to him the other also." (Matthew 5:38-39)**, does this mean that Jews were taught incorrectly? How could one religion state something that is later reversed by a complementing religion? Unfortunately, the principle of "an eye for an eye" is interpreted as meaning you should take revenge with your own hands, but this is not necessarily what the saying meant. The cause and effect (action and reaction) are automatic, and even after many, many incarnations, the effect or reaction may present itself as an opportunity to settle the account with the individual that caused you harm in the first place. Once this opportunity arrives, you may be avenged, and the requirements of the just universal system that we live under will be satisfied. This is not an invitation to violence; the settling of accounts could manifest itself in the form of an "accident," (that is, an event that is prearranged by supernatural forces), without the knowledge of the individuals involved. In some cases, the opportunity to inflict harm is presented in the form of a choice, and when such an opportunity arises, it is up to us to follow Christ's teaching and forgive. In so doing, we elevate our spirits to a higher level.

A country permits an individual to become a leader, and during his or her rule, the country either regresses or prospers. That the individual becomes a leader is not a random occurrence. The people of that country deserve to have that leader. For example, Abraham

Lincoln lead the United States during a period of bloody civil war, but, as a result, the Union was preserved, and the evil of slavery was abolished. The United States deserved to have a leader like him. As a result, the country later prospered, to become the greatest nation on Earth. It is hard to envision how it would have turned out if the North had lost the Civil War, or if the secession from the Union had gone unchallenged.

Now consider the example of Adolf Hitler, who stirred up his nation with astonishing speeches about nationalism and started a war that, in the end, killed millions and devastated Europe —especially Germany, his homeland. How could Hitler have been permitted to do so much harm if the people did not deserve this fate? Does this mean that he was an evil man? There is no way to tell with absolute certainty. To us, it seems that World War II was an unfortunate random happening, but, in reality, it was no more than a vast and carefully executed plan that originated from the Divine Power.

If you recall from your reading of the Old Testament, when the Israelites became evil and worshiped the gods of others, other nations were allowed to conquer them, killing tens of thousands and inflicting pain, slavery, and hardship on the Israelites. If we accept these events as having been staged by God, why should we have a problem accepting that other wars were staged as well?

What have the people of the ex-Soviet Union done to deserve almost 75 years of repressed freedom, sub-standard economic conditions, and the purges of millions of their citizens by Stalin? Only the Almighty knows; however, if these people hadn't deviated —in this or a previous life— from righteous living and behavior, none of these things would have happened to them.

The behavior that lead to the unfortunate circumstances may not have originated from within the boundaries of that country. For example, a U.S. citizen may have done many evil things in life, and, as a partial punishment, the individual may spend his or her next life in a country of repressed freedom, such as the former Soviet Union.

Where do we draw the line between what is predestined and what is not? If humans remembered their previous life or lives, it would be easier, but we don't. If an individual decides to drink or to take drugs, later drives a car, and gets involved in an accident which severely injures the driver of another car, does it mean the other driver "deserved" to be injured? Not necessarily. The drunk or the drug addict inflicted harm on another individual, and, as a result, universal justice will be served in this life or in the life or lives to come. Do you think that drinking to excess was forbidden by all religions for no reason? When an individual purposely loses control over his or her consciousness and commits acts that harm others, that individual is responsible for such actions.

Some may protest, "What is the harm in drinking or using drugs in the privacy of our homes, where no harm is likely to come to anyone?" First, numbing your feelings to escape reality is not a solution, and second, many children throughout history have gone to bed hungry or unclothed because their parents threw their money away on gambling, drugs, and alcohol. This money could have been used to buy food and clothing. There is nothing wrong with the moderate consumption of light alcoholic beverages, especially with meals. After all, Christ turned water into wine and later consumed wine with his disciples during the Last Supper. However, to waste money on meaningless vices is inappropriate even though we may not hurt anyone. Such monies would be better spent on needy people.

Suppose you are driving a car and, all of a sudden, a cat crosses the street directly in front of you. Do you slam on the brakes and try to avoid killing it? Or do you continue driving as if the cat were an insignificant thing? If you try your best to avoid running over the cat, and you fail, you are not to be blamed. That's probably the way things were destined to happen. If you succeed in avoiding it, you feel good, and you thank God that the animal's death is not on your conscience. However, if you don't attempt to miss the cat, you are most likely to be held responsible and to receive some sort of punishment later. Sometimes, people don't realize that a cat has as much right to live as any human being, that it may have kittens depending on it for survival, or that it may belong to people who are very attached to it. Even if it were a wild animal rather than a cat that you were about to hit, things would be no different.

An individual may be in good health and live comfortably. This individual may marry, and soon, one disaster after another is inflicted on him or her, filling the individual's heart with sadness. For another individual, the opposite happens when he or she marries: Poverty is replaced with prosperity, and happiness fills the individual's heart. Is there a relationship between these marriages and the dramatic change in the life of each of these individuals? In my opinion, there is.

When people get married or when they engage in sexual relations, they automatically share some of the spiritual fluids that make each individual unique in life. Thus, a man's spiritual fluids will influence a woman's, and hers will influence him. This influence can be positive, negative, or both. It is quite possible to be positively influenced in certain respects, and, at the same time, negatively influenced in others. The common saying "Behind every great man, there is a woman" should, in my opinion, be replaced with "Behind every great man, there is a woman; behind every great woman, a man; behind every miserable man, a woman; behind every miserable woman, a man."

This is not meant to be an open attack on marriage, because, whether we like it or not, the life of a man or a woman in the absence of the other can be very empty and painful. At the same time, attempting to find a mate that is compatible with your spiritual fluids is a waste of time. Spiritual fluids are not visible, nor are they something you can research.

No one knows how a marriage is going to influence your life or the many lives to come. The system of cause and effect also applies to marriages. For example, if your spouse committed horrible deeds in a previous life, and, as a result, he or she becomes completely paralyzed during your marriage, you may have to spend a large portion of your income on medical bills. In addition to the financial burden, can you imagine how much pain your spouse's suffering would cause you, even though you had nothing to do with his or her past deeds? Of course, you could play it safe and never get married, but that would be a personal choice. **"Now concerning the things where-of ye wrote unto me: It is good for a man not to touch a woman." (1 Corinthians 7:1).**

The other negative side of a marriage is the presence of children. When you have children, whether you like it or not, you take on the responsibility of bringing them into this world to satisfy your selfish desire to be a father or a mother. Your children will naturally inherit many traits (spiritual fluids) from you and your spouse; however, they will eventually set their own course in life, and they may turn out to be decent human beings, or they may turn out to be "the scum of the earth." Having children can be problematic for two reasons. First, you are spiritually responsible to a certain point for their behavior, and they may indirectly hinder your own spiritual progression because they are an extension of you. Second, children may cause you and your spouse pain when they go astray.

Ignorant people argue that it is a moral duty to reproduce, that it is important for someone to carry on the family name and take care of you in your old age. My response to them is "nonsense." At one time, it was important for people to reproduce and populate the Earth; however, if you look around, you will realize that the Earth's population will soon reach 10 billion. If you think that pollution, disposal of wastes, acid rain, and the depletion of the ozone layer are bad right now, just think how much worse they could get. Besides, isn't it more noble when you have selfish desires to become a parent to find and adopt a homeless or abandoned child and provide the child with a better life? In Brazil, for example, there are some three million homeless children who are forced to become involved in shameful and illegal acts in order to survive.

The point I am trying to make is this: As individuals, our life at one time could have begun as "all choice." After one or more incarnations, the choices of one life become the destiny of another. In other words, our life is sometimes controlled by predestined incidents that are nothing but the results of our previous actions, and there is nothing we can do about them, because universal justice must be served. On the other hand, part of our life is controlled by the choices of others. This is obvious when another individual inflicts harm on us for no reason. Finally, many of the actions in our life are nothing but our own clear choices. The hardest part is to distinguish between who is hurting us as an action of his clear choice and who is hurting us as the result of the choices we made in our previous life or lives. Since we don't know which is which, we should not be rushing to place the blame.

A non-literal translation of an old Middle-Eastern saying explains this clearly: "Don't get too upset because of a mishap, for it may have happened for your own good." As an example, you may lose your car keys and spend 10 minutes looking for them in every possible place. Finally, you find them and wonder how they got there. You may become angry because you are now running late, but what if this incident was pre-arranged for a reason? Suppose that if you had not been detained for these 10 minutes, somebody would have harmed you in some way out of free choice, but because you "deserved" to be rescued, some divine intervention was necessary? How would you feel about your lost keys now?

At times, you may find yourself in a difficult situation, with no one likely to help, but somehow, a total stranger appears at the right moment and helps you out. Certainly, there are many "good Samaritans" on Earth, but how did it happen that such an individual was present at the right time and place? Could it be that this individual was "inspired" to be there so you would receive help? Could this person be repaying a debt to you from another life? How can we be sure that such an individual is just another human being like you and me?

What if this individual doesn't really exist but is a transfiguration of a supernatural entity?

People tend to rule out intervention from the spiritual world because it doesn't appear likely or even possible to them. When people think of the spiritual world, they often think of fiery flames, angels emitting blinding white light, and awesome and powerful voices. But the spiritual world is not necessarily like that. The "angels" that appeared in human form to help Lot and his family flee Sodom and Gomorrah looked no different from any other human being. Actually, they were so real that the people of that time lusted after them: **"And there came two angels to Sodom at even; and Lot sat in the gate of Sodom: and Lot seeing them rose up to meet them; and he bowed himself with his face toward the ground; and he said, Behold now, my lords, turn in, I pray you, into your servant's house, and tarry all night, and wash your feet, and ye shall rise up early, and go on your ways. And they said, Nay; but we will abide in the street all night. And he pressed upon them greatly; and they turned in unto him, and entered into his house;** *and he made them a feast, and did bake unleavened bread, and they did eat.* **But before they lay down, the men of the city, even the men of Sodom, compassed the house round, both old and young, all the people from every quarter: And they called unto Lot, and said unto him,** *Where are the men which came in to thee this night? bring them out unto us, that we may know them.* **And Lot went out at the door unto them, and shut the door after him, And said, I pray you, brethren, do not so wickedly. Behold now, I have two daughters which have not known man; let me, I pray you, bring them out unto you and do ye to them as is good in your eyes: only unto these** men do nothing; for therefore came they under the shadow of my roof." (Genesis 19:1-8).

What about the "man" that Jacob wrestled with all night, only to discover that he was really an angel of God? **"And Jacob was left alone; and there wrestled a man with him until the breaking of the day. And when he saw that he prevailed not against him, he touched the hollow of his thigh; and the hollow of Jacob's thigh was out of joint, as he wrestled with him. And he said, Let me go, for the day breaketh. And he said, I will not let thee go, except thou bless me. And he said unto him, What is thy name? And he said, Jacob. And he said, Thy name shall be called no more Jacob, but Israel: for as a prince hast thou power with God and with men, and hast prevailed." (Genesis 32:24-29).**

A popular story from the early Christian era tells about a group of Christians who hid in a cave to escape death by the Romans. They prayed fervently that their lives would be spared, and God answered their prayers by causing them to sleep for 309 years. Once they woke up, they noticed nothing unusual; however, when they were forced to leave the cave to seek food, they were shocked to discover that Christianity was by then widespread and that the people they once knew were no longer alive. After talking to the people they encountered, they learned that it had been 309 years since they had disappeared.

The Koran corroborates this story: **"Behold, the youths betook themselves to the Cave: they said "Our Lord! bestow on us mercy from Thyself and dispose of our affair for us in the right way!" Then We draw (a veil) over their ears, for a number of** years, in the Cave (So that they heard not): Then We roused them, in order to test which of the two parties was best at calculating the term of years they had tarried! We relate to thee their story in truth: they were youths who believed in their Lord, and We advanced them in guidance: We gave strength to their hearts:... Thou wouldst have deemed them awake, whilst they were asleep, and We turned them on their right and on their left sides: their dog stretching forth his two fore-legs on the threshold: if thou hadst come up on to them, thou wouldst have certainly turned back from them in flight, and wouldst certainly have been filled with terror of them. Such (being their state), We raised them up (from sleep), that they might question each other. Said one of them, 'How long have ye stayed (here)?' They said, 'We have stayed (Perhaps) a day, or part of a day' (At length) they (all) said, 'God (alone) knows best how long ye have stayed here...Thus did We make their case known to the people,...So they stayed in their Cave three hundred years, and (some) add nine (more).' " (Sura XVIII: Kahf 10-25).

If there is a scientific explanation for this occurrence, how could such an incident have taken place 1600 years ago, especially when it is not even possible to prolong life in this manner with our best technology, unless supernatural forces truly intervened?

How could Daniel have survived in the den of wild lions? **"My God hath sent his angel, and hath shut the lions' mouths, that they have not hurt me: forasmuch as before him innocency was found in me; and also before thee, O king, have I done no hurt."** (Daniel 6:22).

These and many other incidents throughout the Holy Books tend to reinforce the idea of intervention by supernatural forces. But some incidents may not be so supernatural after all. Consider, for example, how Ezekiel described his vision of the Cherubim: **"And I looked, and, behold, a whirlwind came out of the north, a great cloud, and a fire infolding itself, and a brightness was about it, and out of the midst thereof as the color of amber, out of the midst of the fire... And their feet were straight feet; and the sole of their feet was like the sole of a calf's foot: and they sparkled like the color of burnished brass...and their wings were stretched upward; two wings of every one were joined one to another, and two covered their bodies... their appearance was like burning coals of fire, and like the appearance of lamps: it went up and down among the living creatures; and the fire was bright, and out of the fire went forth lightning...and their rings were full of eyes round about them four. And when the living creatures went, the wheels went by them: and when the living creatures were lifted up from the earth, the wheels were lifted up ... And when they went, I heard the noise of their wings, like the noise of great waters, as the voice of the Almighty, the voice of speech, as the noise of a host: when they stood, they let down their wings. And there was a voice from the firmament that was over their heads, when they stood, and had let down their wings...And when I saw it, I fell upon my face, and I heard a voice of one that spake." (Ezekiel 1:4-28).** If Ezekiel saw an airplane at that time, do you think that he would have described it as a machine, or as a beast that looked like a bird? What if his vision was simply a description of a space ship?

How could Jonah have survived for three days inside a living whale? **"Now the Lord had prepared a great fish to swallow up Jonah. And Jonah was in the belly of the fish three days and three nights." (Jonah 1:17). "And the Lord spake unto the fish, and it vomited out Jonah upon the dry land." (Jonah 2:10).** Could any scientist demonstrate that a human being has a chance of surviving inside the digestive system of a whale for three full days in the absence of oxygen and still come out intact? How would an individual from that time describe a submarine if he saw one? Would he have described it as a machine, or as a great fish?

Consider this passage also: **"And it came to pass, when they were gone over, that Elijah said unto Elisha, Ask what I shall do for thee, before I be taken away from thee. And Elisha said, I pray thee, let a double portion of thy spirit be upon me. And he said, Thou has asked hard things: nevertheless, if thou see me when I am taken from thee, it shall be so unto thee; but if not, it shall not be so. And it came to pass, as they still went on, and talked, that, behold, *there appeared a chariot of fire, and horses of fire*, and parted them both asunder; and Elijah went up by a whirlwind into heaven." (2 Kings 2:9-11).** If the Divine Power wanted to claim Elijah back, wouldn't a simple disappearance have done the trick? Why orchestrate a departure that includes a chariot of fire that took Elijah to heaven in a whirlwind, unless the chariot was a primitive man's way of describing a space ship?

The point that I am trying to make is this: Certain incidents from the Holy Books seem to be nonsense if scrutinized and interpreted literally by a rational twentieth century human being. However, if these incidents are analyzed in a wider context, they become probable.

CHAPTER 5

THE FINAL DAYS

Holy Books speak of the Judgment Day or Doom's Day and give signs about when this day will come. This day would bring an end to the current life cycle on Earth and begin another; however, the next life cycle would not necessarily begin immediately after the current life cycle. It may take thousands or even millions of years for a new cycle to begin.

Such would be the case if a wide-scale nuclear war were to take place, creating deadly radiation that would prohibit life on Earth for a long time. Or the next life cycle may actually begin immediately after the current life cycle. Just as the current life cycle began with Noah and his family following the Flood, with only the handful of people and animals that survived and re-populated the Earth, it is possible for a similar transition to take place. But it is not likely.

"And as it was in the days of Noah, so shall it be also in the days of the Son of man. They did eat, they drank, they married wives, they were given in marriage, until the day that Noah entered into the ark, and the flood came, and destroyed them all. Likewise also as it was in the days of Lot; they did eat, they drank, they bought, they sold, they planted, they builded; but the same day that Lot

went out of Sodom it rained fire and brimstone from heaven, and destroyed them all." (Luke 17:26-29). "Generations before you we destroyed when they did wrong: their Apostles came to them with Clear Signs, but they would not believe! Thus do We requite those who sin! Then We made you heirs in the land after them, to see how ye would behave! (Sura X: Yunus 13:14). "The day that We roll up the heavens like a scroll rolled up for books (completed), —*Even as We produced the first Creation, so shall We produce a new one: a promise We have undertaken: Truly shall We fulfil it.* Before this We wrote in the Psalms, after the Message (given to Moses): 'My servants, the righteous, shall inherit the earth.' " (Sura XXI: Anbiyãa 104-105). "Behold, the Lord maketh the earth empty, and maketh it waste, and turneth it upside down, and scattereth abroad the inhabitants thereof...The land shall be utterly emptied and utterly spoiled: for the Lord hath spoken this word. The earth mourneth and fadeth away, the world languisheth and fadeth away, the haughty people of the earth do languish. The earth also is defiled under the inhabitants thereof; because they have transgressed the laws, changed the ordinance, broken the everlasting covenant." (Isaiah 24:1-5).

The Earth has gone through many life cycles. During these life cycles, the inhabitants of the Earth reach a certain level of evil and wickedness, despite the warnings of the prophets of their time, making it necessary for the Creator to destroy civilization and start over. All signs lead me to believe that the current life cycle is about to end. All the signs in the Holy Books are coming true: **"Now the brother shall betray the brother to death, and the father the son; and children shall rise up** against their parents, and shall cause them to be put to death." (Mark 13:12). "For nation shall rise against nation, and kingdom against kingdom; and there shall be famines, and pestilences, and earthquakes, in divers places. All these are the beginning of sorrows. Then shall they deliver you up to be afflicted, and shall kill you; and ye shall be hated of all nations for my name's sake. And then shall many be offended and shall betray one another, and shall hate one another. *And many false prophets shall rise, and shall deceive many.* And because iniquity shall abound, the love of many shall wax cold. But he that shall endure unto the end, the same shall be saved. *And this gospel of the kingdom shall be preached in all the world for a witness unto all nations; and then shall the end come.*" (Matthew 24:7-14).

The world has become very materialistic. People would do just about anything for money. Our life has become a very confused existence. True friends are rare if not non-existent. Today, so-called friends are attached to each other by selfish materialistic or personal needs. True love is equally as rare, and most marriages are based on physical needs and economic arrangements. The wickedness on Earth is increasing, morality is declining, and sexual deviation and promiscuity have become an acceptable part of life for the majority, far exceeding the immorality of the people of Sodom and Gomorrah. Some churches have begun performing marriage ceremonies for homosexual male or lesbian couples. **"This know also, that in the last days perilous times shall come. For men shall be lovers of their own selves, covetous, boasters, proud, blasphemers, disobedient to parents, unthankful, unholy, without natural affection, truce breakers, false accusers, inconti-**

nent, fierce, despisers of those that are good, traitors, heady, high-minded, lovers of pleasures more than lovers of God; having a form of godliness, but denying the power thereof: from such turn away. For of this sort are they which creep into houses, and lead captive silly women laden with sins, led away with divers lusts, ever learning, and never able to come to the knowledge of the truth." (2 Timothy 3:1-7).

Diseases such as cancer and AIDS are spreading, the environment is being destroyed by acid rain, pollution, and other abuses of the human race, and the ozone layer is deteriorating. When the Earth's population doubles in a few years, such problems will become even more pronounced. Our self-destruction is becoming increasingly likely.

The justice system world-wide is at times very biased and heavily influenced by political or religious groups; at other times, it is absolutely corrupt. Consider, for example, the incident that led to the riots in Los Angeles in April 1992, in which more than 50 people were killed, hundreds injured, and a large area of central Los Angeles destroyed —all due to the acquittal by jury of four police officers on a charge of beating a Black motorist, despite the fact that the brutal beating was recorded on a video tape that had been broadcast world-wide on television news.

Or consider some of the decisions made by the United Nations, where a system of double standards is regularly applied and controlled by the major players, the Super Powers. Why didn't the United Nations condemn the United States for human rights violations in the 1960's when Blacks were treated as sub-citizens, denied their voting rights? Imagine: Only 30 years ago, the most advanced and powerful country in the World tolerated such injustices. Where was the United Nations when the United States invaded Panama or Grenada? Why didn't the United Nations send troops to Afghanistan when it was invaded by the Soviet Union? Why did the United Nations force Iraq out of Kuwait but has not forced Israel out of the West Bank? I am not citing these examples for any political reason, nor to voice my position on any issues. Rather, I want to show that human justice is not always served and that we should not be fooled by appearances.

We are in a very dangerous period, a time in which it is possible for an extremist to possess nuclear weapons or to become the leader of a nation that is capable of building nuclear weapons of mass destruction. **"Immediately after the tribulation of those days shall the sun be darkened, and the moon shall not give her light..." (Matthew 24:29). "But the day of the Lord will come as a thief in the night; in the which the heavens shall pass away with a great noise,** *and the elements shall melt with fervent heat*, **the earth also and the works that are therein shall be burned up." (1 Peter 3:10).**

According to the scientist Carl Sagan, in the aftermath of a nuclear war, the dust and smoke from the explosions will remain in the atmosphere for a long time and block the sun's rays from reaching the surface of the planet. This will prevent the Earth's surface from absorbing heat, and a phenomenon called "Nuclear Winter" will take place. Temperatures will plummet, making the Earth's atmosphere far less conducive to life. If there are people who survive the immediate destruction and radiation of a wide-scale nuclear disaster, they may not survive Nuclear Winter.

Some people may wonder why destruction is inevitable. Remember that this life is nothing but a small chapter in our existence and that we have been given "another chance," many, many times; however, without a change in our attitude and behavior, there may come a time when continued life on Earth becomes counter-productive. If the present decline in morality is any indication, most people have already regressed. Another thing to keep in mind is that, with the continued abuse of nature, it may be very difficult for the Earth to support life without further and more severe hardships, whether these come in the form of the rapid spread of disease or respiratory and physical failures caused by polluted air, water, and food. Total destruction of the Earth could really be a merciful act from God. Let's hope that when total destruction comes, it happens quickly enough to minimize our suffering.

Given what has been discussed earlier in this chapter and in the previous chapters, the question that comes to mind is how should an individual behave at this age, until the end of this life cycle? Clearly, there is no set of rules written anywhere, nor is there a magical formula that can be applied.

On a personal level, I find it necessary to base my life upon a set of rational principles derived from my life experiences and my philosophical beliefs. Most of these principles are consistent with the teachings of all religions, but some of them deviate entirely from religious teachings. Here are my personal principles:

1-Believe in a Creator, the only Creator, by whatever name, Allah, God, or any other name given to the

Creative Force. **"God is He who created seven Firmaments and of the earth a similar number. Through the midst of them (all) descends His command: that ye may know that God has power over all things, and that God comprehends all things in (His) Knowledge." (Sura LXV: Talaq 12). "The great God that formed all things both rewardeth the fool, and rewardeth transgressors." (Proverbs 26:10).**

2-Believe in all the prophets of God (Christ, Moses, Mohammed, Gandhi, Buddha, Dahesh, and many others). **"To every people (was sent) an Apostle: when their Apostle comes (before them), the matter will be judged between them with justice, and they will not be wronged." (Sura X: Yunis 47).**

3-Believe in the essence of any religion that is founded on the Ten Commandments. Respect these religions, and always keep in mind that some religions are more mature than others. Do not be concerned with nor involved in their rituals or their method of prayer.

When asked what my religion is, I reply that I am a Jew, a Christian, a Moslem, and a follower of many other faiths, all in one, for I am a Daheshist. Once you understand that the essence of a religion is what really counts, your attitude toward other religions will change. When an individual understands this, he or she can work to crush the religious barriers that lead nations to war or to mend the wounds of a civil war fueled by religious hatred. **"The same religion has He established for you as that which He enjoined on Noah —the which we have sent**

by inspiration to thee —and that which we enjoined on Abraham, Moses, and Jesus: Namely, that ye should remain steadfast in religion, and make no divisions therein..." (Sura XLII: Shura 13).

4- Use money only as a means for purchasing the necessities of life. Do not seek treasures in this life. Human greed is an ugly trait, and no matter how much money or material assets the greedy individual collects, he or she still yearns for more. Unfortunately, we live in a material world where we must use money to survive or to achieve certain goals (such as publishing, printing, and distributing this book). Hypothetically, it would be wonderful to live in a pure Socialist environment; however, in reality, such a system doesn't work.

5- Refuse to participate in sectarianism. It is better not to attend any church, mosque, synagogue, or temple of a religion that claims to be above other religions. Such organizations are economic entities that are pulling people away from the true faith.

If you ask me, the leaders of these so-called religious entities represent a "den of robbers" and are no different from the traders that Christ chased away from the Temple. They are false prophets. Many of the Christian clergy like to be called "Father," in direct disobedience to Christ's teachings. **"But be not ye called Rabbi: for one is your Master, even Christ, and all ye are brethren. And call no man your Father upon the earth: for one is your Father, which is in heaven. Neither be ye called masters: for one is your Master, even Christ." (Matthew 23:8-10).**

They build structures in the name of God; however, they use them as palaces for their own selfish living. They claim deity and purity, while in reality they are more tainted than the people they purport to lead. How dare these religious leaders take money from the poor and use it to buy wine and feasts for themselves? How many of these "pious" men and women have, ironically, carried on illicit love affairs, while preaching chastity? How many bastards have the supposedly chaste clergy fathered or borne in this life? What about the crooked evangelists that claim to heal and perform miracles on paid TV to collect money?

Scandals such as the immorality and financial misconduct of Jim Bakker and the confessed promiscuity of Jimmy Swaggart are only recent examples of the corruption of the clergy throughout history. **"O ye who believe! There are indeed many among the priests and anchorites, who in falsehood devour the substance of men and hinder (them) from the Way of God. And there are those who bury gold and silver and spend it not in the Way of God: announce unto them a most grievous penalty." (Sura IX: Tauba 34). "And many false prophets shall rise, and shall deceive many." (Matthew 24:11).**

"Little children, it is the last time: and as ye have heard that antichrist shall come, even now are there many antichrists; whereby we know that it is the last time. They went out from us, but they were not of us; for if they had been of us, they would no doubt have continued with us: but they went out, that they might be made manifest that they were not all of us." (1 John 2:18-19).

6-Deal with people in fairness. Knowing that cheating, theft, and dishonesty are shunned by all religions, and that for every such act punishment will follow, either in this life or the lives to come, abstain from such acts, do what is righteous, and leave the rest to Divine Justice.

7-Have compassion toward the poor, homeless, hungry, and the sick of this world. If you can lend a helping hand, do so, despite your understanding that these people "deserved" to be in this situation because of their deeds in this or a previous life. Money spent on noble causes is always better than money spent to procure weapons of destruction, to subsidize selfish entertainment, or to fuel conflicts. Show similar compassion toward all living creatures.

8-Do not deny your faith, no matter what the consequences may be. What would life be worth if you had no principles to live for? Would you be satisfied with eating, drinking, and sleeping? If you see injustice, stand up and fight it. If you see evil, condemn it.

9-Seek knowledge continually. Ignorance doesn't do you any good if your goal is to seek spiritual advancement. Study, analyze, and debate subjects that pertain to your existence, and act upon the knowledge you gain. The world of art, poetry, and literature is full of implicit and explicit emotions, thought-provoking stories, and rich sensory experiences that can refine you. Good classical music can touch your heart and lessen the pains of this life. Science presents challenges that can stretch your imagination and strengthen your problem-solving abilities.

10-Seek to improve morality by abstaining from the evil things in life. Avoid evil groups, because "bad apples spoil good apples." Sexual promiscuity and sexual deviation are unacceptable. Abstain from drugs and excessive drinking, which make an individual lose control over his or her consciousness, and leads the individual to commit disgraceful acts or harm others.

11-Do not hesitate to help others if it is within your means. Act as a good Samaritan. If your relative, neighbor, or even a stranger is in need of help, financial or non-financial, it is your moral duty to help discretely when you can.

12-Have no ambitions for personal glory. What is the point of glory? To earn a place in history for having lived? Once you die, you take with you only the deeds you have performed, nothing else. Modesty is a virtue.

13-Do not condone or resort to physical violence. If logic doesn't resolve a dispute, drop the subject, or rely on the legal system, no matter how imperfect it is, or leave the resolution to the just universal system. Self-defense is different and is a matter of personal choice.

14-Do not judge others. No one is perfect, and those who claim to be are fools. If you accuse an individual of a wrongful act, you should be absolutely sure that, in the same situation, you would not do the same thing. In general, it is better not to judge others.

15-Do not be sexist or racist. With the exception of

some physical differences, there should be no differentiation between men and women. Each individual should be evaluated on the basis of his or her intelligence and behavior. It makes no difference if an individual is White, Black, Red, male, female, Christian, Moslem, Jewish, Hindu, or a member of any other race or ethnic group. **"Have we not all one father? hath not one God created us? why do we deal treacherously every man against his brother, by profaning the covenant of our fathers?" (Malachi 2:10).**

16- Do not believe in sorcery, magic, telekinesis, telepathy, hypnosis, palmistry, or horoscopes. They are all without substance. No one, other than God and possibly his prophets, has the power to know the past or present of another soul, nor the ability to violate the laws of the Universe. No one can control your mind and force you to do anything against your free will. Suggestive compliance is a sign of mental weakness.

17- Do not believe in superficial things such as makeup, tanning, and jewelry. Your taste in clothing should be conservative. Your body is not a display case, so don't go around showing off. You don't need to buy expensive clothing: this is a waste.

18- It is not sufficient to hold onto your beliefs. Rather, if you are firmly convinced of their validity, pass them along to others, in a way that they will understand, so that they also can be enlightened. What good does it do to publish a book if no one else can read it? It is our duty to fight the forces of darkness so that others can benefit, and so that your spirit will advance.

19-Forgive whenever you can, and practice the commandment **"Love thy neighbor."**

20-Pray to Almighty God. **"And when thou prayest, thou shalt not be as the hypocrites are: for they love to pray standing in the synagogues and in the corners of the streets, that they may be seen of men. Verily I say unto you, They have their reward. But thou, when thou prayest, enter into thy closet and when thou hast shut thy door, pray to thy Father which is in secret; and thy Father which seeth in secret shall reward thee openly." (Matthew 6:5-6).**

Your comments and questions are welcome. Please send all correspondence to the author at the following address:

>Murad Publishing
>P.O. Box 16680
>Alexandria, Virginia 22302-8680

REFERENCES

Davies, Paul and Gribbin, John (1992)
    "The Matter Myth"
    New York: Touchstone Book

Hartmann, William (1991)
    "The History of Earth"
    New York: Workman Publishing Company, Inc.

Hawking, Stephen (1988)
    "A Brief History of Time"
    New York: Bantam Books

Lightman, Alan (1992)
    "Time for the Stars"
    New York: Viking Penguin

Trefil, James (1989)
    "Reading the Mind of God"
    New York: Anchor Books

Holy Bible, The King James Version

Holy Qur'an, A translation by A. Yusuf Ali